The Gospel of Joy in America

*Landscape and Priorities
for Evangelization in the United States
in the Twenty-First Century*

Hosffman Ospino, PhD

CONVIVIUM**PRESS**
2018

Convivium Press, 2018
© Hosffman Ospino
All rights reserved

http://www.conviviumpress.com
sales@conviviumpress.com
ventas@conviviumpress.com
convivium@conviviumpress.com

7661 nw 68th St, Suite 108
Miami, Florida 33166. usa
Phone: +1 (305) 8890489
Fax: +1 (305) 8875463

isbn: 978-1-934996-69-0

Written *by* Hosffman Ospino

Designed *by* Eduardo Chumaceiro d'E
graphicbureau@yahoo.com

Printed in Colombia
Impreso en Colombia
Panamericana Formas e Impresos S.A.

Convivium Press
Miami, 2018

No part of this book may be reproduced
or utilized in any form or by any means, electronic
or mechanical, including photocopying and
recording, or by any information storage or retrieval
system, without permission in writing from
the publisher.

Introduction

Catholicism in the United States during the twenty-first century will be defined by the passion and the commitment of all who accept the invitation to be authentic missionary disciples of Jesus Christ. We follow in the footsteps of countless Catholics who preceded us building communities and keeping the faith alive. It is our turn. We do this aware of our strengths and limitations as well as our hopes and anxieties. We do this as a body of diverse souls and hearts that profess the same faith with joy and seek communion with God and with one another. Ours is truly a Catholic moment.

This inspirational reflection was delivered by Catholic theologian, Dr. Hosffman Ospino, as the opening keynote on Sunday, July 2, 2017 before thousands of Catholic leaders participating in the *Convocation of Catholic Leaders: The Joy of the Gospel in America*, organized by the United States Conference of Catholic Bishops (USCCB).

How to best
read,
& reflect,
discuss

this short text?

- Procure copies to share with others in your family and in your faith community. Read in small groups (it will not take you more than 20 minutes!).

- Share your reactions. Use the questions at the end.

- Reimagine your personal commitment or your particular ministry in light of the insights here.

The Gospel of *Joy* in America

What a wonderful time to be Catholic in the United States of America! Please join me praising the Lord by saying together a resounding amen:

Amen!

Yes,
amen,
we
are
here

We come together to engage in a very important exercise of "**evangelical discernment,**" as Pope Francis reminds us.

(THE JOY OF THE GOSPEL, N. 50)

God calls us to respond
to the invitation to reflect
intentionally about
what it means to be missionary
disciples of Jesus Christ
proclaiming the

Joy

of the Gospel in every corner
of our nation.

What will Catholics a hundred years from now
remember about us when they look back
at the first decades of the twenty-first century?

How will historians define the
historical period in which you and I live?
What will be our legacy?

What kind of faith communities
will our children and grandchildren
inherit?

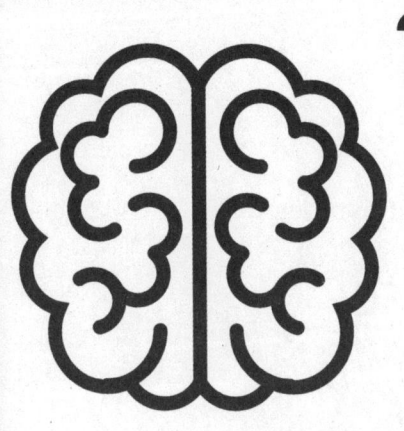

?

These questions
often hunt
my imagination.

Although we cannot control
what historians of U.S. Catholicism
will write in one hundred years,
we can definitely give them the best
stories, our stories and those
of our communities.

I believe that this is why
God calls to be part of this reflection:

to set the course
of what can be
a new Catholic moment
in the United States.

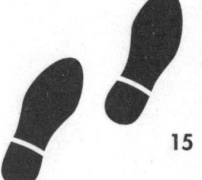

It is imperative that we have the best possible
understanding of who we are as Catholics
in the United States and the particular contexts
in which we live and practice our faith.
Allow me to walk with you sharing a few thoughts
in this regard.

The large waves of Catholic immigrants arriving mainly from Western Europe during the nineteenth century quickly eclipsed the influence of the small Catholic settlements established during colonial times that preceded the birth of our nation. Many of these early communities were Hispanic and French.

In a period of roughly 150 years,
the new Catholic immigrants
built more than

> 20,000 parishes,

more than

> 13,000 schools,

hundreds of

> universities,
> hospitals,

and massive networks
of social services.

Such presence eventually
led to a strong

political,
& cultural,
intellectual presence

in the public square.

The rapid growth of Catholicism
in such a short period of time
was unprecedented, actually dazzling,
a true miracle considering the socio-political
circumstances that these Catholic sisters
and brothers had to face, including major bouts
of anti-Catholic sentiment.

Much of what identifies
U.S. Catholicism today
is the result of those years
of growth defined by
a strong Euro-American
cultural heritage.

Toward the middle of the twentieth century,
U.S. Catholicism had entered a relatively brief
period of stability. Most European immigrants
had settled and their U.S. born children
and grandchildren were quickly embracing the

"American way of Life"

U.S. Catholics had been
engaged in a long process of

soul-searching

about whether they should be
more Catholic or more American.
Eventually most opted
for a both/end solution to
the dilemma.

> Millions of U.S. Catholics
> became highly educated; many
> joined the middle and
> upper classes of our society.

A large number of ethnic churches that welcomed immigrants from many parts of the world and served as oases to support faith and culture, eventually transitioned to serve wider bodies of Catholics in English; some of these churches ceased to exist as their mission ended.

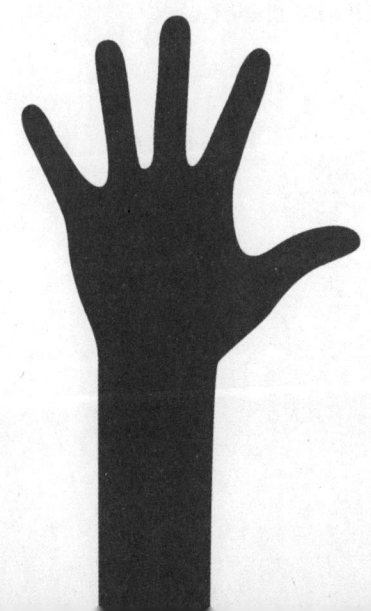

If the history of U.S. Catholicism had stopped at this particular moment, we could offer this communal experience as a perfect case study of the American Dream achieved. Yet, history moves along. Some important changes were in store.

Before we move on, we need to understand that not all U.S. Catholics participated of this upward movement nor benefitted from the wealth of resources that Euro-American Catholic communities were creating. African-American, Hispanic, Native American, and Asian American Catholics largely remained in the peripheries of church and society.

We cannot naively
ignore the fact
that socio-cultural prejudices
such as

& racism

classism

have done major harm
to millions of our own Catholic
sisters and brothers.

Millions of Euro-American
Catholics in rural areas of the country
were caught up in a cycle of

poverty & marginalization

and were practically forgotten
as the major centers of Catholic life,
particularly in the urban settings
of the Northeast and Midwest thrived.

{ Ironically, it is these communities that inhabited the peripheries of church and society… the voices that for long were not heard… the faces that remained invisible… that are bringing new life to our faith communities and renewing the entire U.S. Catholic experience. }

LET ME SAY MORE
ABOUT THIS.

For the last five decades, U.S. Catholicism has been experiencing the largest demographic and cultural transformation since the time of the large migrations from Europe in the nineteenth and early twentieth centuries.

Hispanics account for 71% of the growth of the Catholic population in the United States since 1960. Approximately 60% of all Catholics younger than 18 are Hispanic.

The fastest-growing group in the Church in this country is Asians Catholics. Hundreds of thousands of Catholics from Africa and the Caribbean have made the U.S. their home.

Millions of the new Catholic faces are
immigrants. They bring the best
of their faith and cultures to enrich our faith
communities and our society. About
a quarter of all Catholics in this country are
immigrants. They and their children
embody the hope of a new beginning.
They have much to teach us about
faith and life.

>
> Immigrants are
> neither the enemy nor a threat; they
> are the face of
> # Christ,
> the living Gospel that
> we are called
> to embrace with merciful
> love and
> Christian hospitality.

If we were to paint a broad picture of U.S. Catholics in the country, this is what the rough demographic portrait would look like:

ABOUT

1% Native American,
4% African-American/Black,
5% Asian and Pacific Islander,
40% Hispanic,

AND ABOUT

50% Euro-American, White.

This is a much different portrait compared to, say, half a century ago when Euro-American White Catholics constituted about 85% to 90% of all Catholics in the country.

Let us look around for a moment.

Turn to your right.

Now to your left.

Based on what we just heard, do we see the faces of present-day U.S. Catholics among us? Do we see them in our faith communities? Do we see them in our diocesan offices and organizations? Do we see them in our Catholic schools, universities, and seminaries? Are we listening to their voices? Do we know their concerns? Are we reaching out? Are they still in the peripheries of our church?

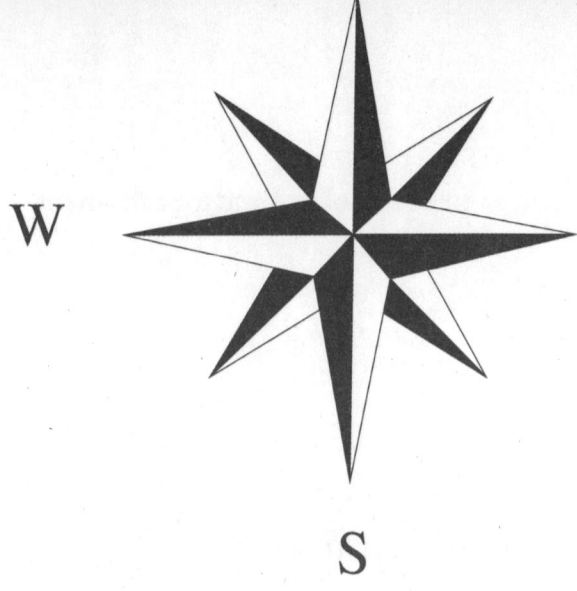

The demographic transformations
of U.S. Catholicism come along with some
geographical shifts that we need to
keep in mind. Today, more than half of Catholics
in the United States live in the South
and the West. The present and the future
of U.S. Catholicism is being forged
in geographical regions that until now were
not perceived as central to the definition
of U.S. Catholic life. Today they are!

We live in a moment in which whatever happens in Los Angeles, Houston, Atlanta, and Miami, among many other large vibrant centers of Catholic life, will likely have significant repercussions for the rest of the Catholic community nationwide.

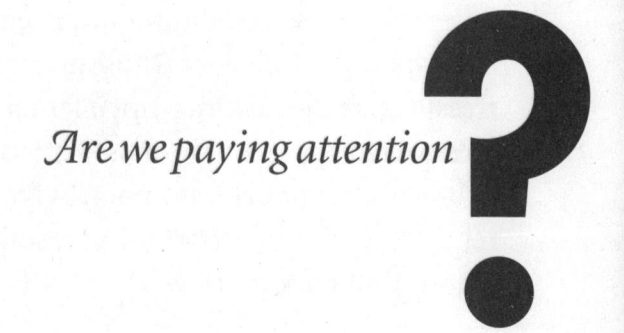

Are we paying attention **?**

Of concern is the fact that the rapid growth of Catholicism in the South and the West does not match the availability of resources such as parishes, schools, universities, and pastoral centers needed to support the evangelization and leadership formation of the next generation of U.S. Catholics.

We are witnessing a transition from a Catholic experience highly resourced and somewhat comfortable in terms of socio-economic positioning, to one shaped strongly by Catholics with fewer resources, less education, and emerging socio-political influence whose greatest treasures are their faith and their families. This is an excellent opportunity for us in this country to be a poor church for the poor, as Pope Francis reminds us, and an opportunity for solidarity among Catholics at all levels.

{ While contending with these demographic and geographical changes in our church, the last half a century has seen the emergence of major cultural patterns that are seriously impacting the practice of religion in our country. }

Among these,
I want to mention
four:

1. **Family life** has been significantly reconfigured in terms of roles, expectations, and practices. If the family is the first space where the new generations learn their faith and the matrix where religious and moral values are cultivated, Catholics must redouble our efforts to engage in critical dialogue about fostering vibrant family life while responding creatively, yet realistically to the challenges of being family in the United States.

2. Our society continues to witness, almost helplessly, the **erosion of communal life.** This has exacerbated our individualistic instincts. If communal life is not important, being with others loses meaning, advocating for others and for shared convictions is not a priority, and caring about those who are most vulnerable becomes someone else's problem.

From a religious perspective, worshipping together is not a priority anymore. It is rather disquieting that barely one third of U.S. Catholics attend Mass on a regular basis. **1/3**

Even more disquieting is to know that the Catholic population has grown by about **50%** in the last half a century, yet we find ourselves closing churches.

3. The so-called "culture wars" have rendered us almost unable in our society to engage in mutual and respectful dialogue. It has become impossible to speak about virtually anything because it is expected that one needs to take an ideological position to make a point… and that practically means demonizing the other who somewhat disagrees with us or does not see the world as we see it. The Gospel is not an ideology to be coopted to advance any personal agenda.

The Gospel is a message of life and communion.

4. Perhaps the most influential phenomenon impacting the practice of religion in our day is **secularization:** in 1991 about 3% of the U.S. population self-identified as non-religiously affiliated or "nones". Today, three decades later, about 25% of all people in our country self-identify as such. The trend is very clear.

> We know that about 20 million people in our country who were born and raised Catholic do not self-identify as such any more. It is likely that many of them, especially those who are young, joined the ranks of the "nones." About 14 million Hispanics born and raised Catholic do not self-identify as such any more. Most of them young and U.S. born. Are they part of the previous 20 million? My sense is that most are not. We have a serious challenge. Why are they leaving? Why is organized religion, particularly Catholicism, not doing it for them? Did we know that they left? If so, where is the outrage?

What do we learn from these observations?
Perhaps the best way to read these realities
is through the lens of two Greek terms well known
in our Christian theological tradition:

Krisis and *Kairós.*

Krisis is understood here in terms of transition. It is the liminal space in between

what is passing & what is coming.

There is no doubt that some ways of being U.S. Catholic are closing their cycle. For them we are grateful.

It is fine that some Catholics feel puzzled when wrestling with diversity and pluralism, disconcerted because of a sense of loss, confused when the future does not seem as clearly defined and stable as we thought it could be —yet neither is our present. This is where we all must exercise the pastoral practice of mutual accompaniment.

It would be naive to seek a return to the past, except to draw some inspiration and lessons for the future. An idealized past does not help much. There is no doubt that we are at the dawn of a fresher way of being Catholic in this country.

(40) At the forefront
of this dawn are our

young catholic people —the majority Hispanic—

with their hopes and the thirst to be
church; the immigrants who bring renewed life
and energy to our faith communities;
the women and the men of all cultures and ages
who are willing to look forward by
serving as bridges to heal divides and the
effects of prejudice in any of its
expressions.

Yes, something new is emerging, a new time, a moment of grace, a *kairós*. We have the certainty that God walks with us and guides us with the Holy Spirit. In this *kairós* we are called to renew the invitation to proclaim the joy of the Gospel in every corner of our nation. To echo the words of the prophet Ezekiel, God has called us from among the nations, and gathered us from all the lands to be God's faithful people (Cf. Ez 36:24-28).

This is a time
for Catholics in the
United States
not only to embrace
the call to being
missionary disciples,
but also to declare
ourselves in a permanent
state of mission.
Let me repeat:

> **we must declare ourselves in a permanent state of mission.**

We must see ourselves permanently engaged in missionary activity, going forth (*en salida*, as Pope Francis says in Spanish), taking the initiative, going to the peripheries, embracing Jesus Christ in those who are vulnerable and most in need, reaching out to those who have drifted away, accompanying and strengthening families, advocating for life in all its expressions, caring for the created order…

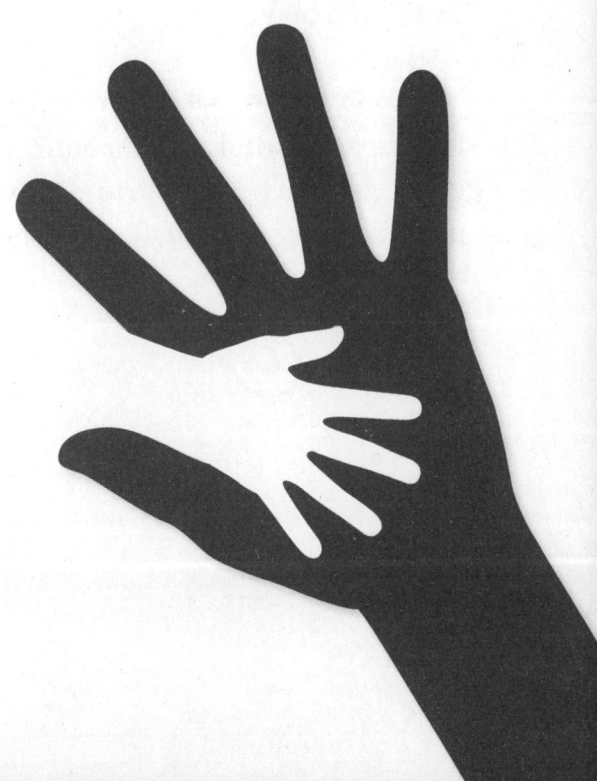

Hundreds of thousands of Hispanic Catholics and others are modeling this commitment presently engaged in a four-year process called the

Fifth National Encuentro of Hispanic/Latino Ministry.

This process of evangelization is not just for Hispanics but also for the entire Church in our country. I invite you to join the process and the spirit of the Fifth Encuentro and make it your own.

When historians a hundred years from now
look back at Catholics in the United States in the
second decade of the twenty-first century,
we should be remembered as a generation of
baptized women and men, disciples
of Jesus Christ…

who decided to build upon the foundations
left by the previous generations, embraced the gifts
of every Catholic person in our communities
—without exception— and accepted to be a true
evangelizing community committed to
building a better society for our children and
future generations of Catholics.

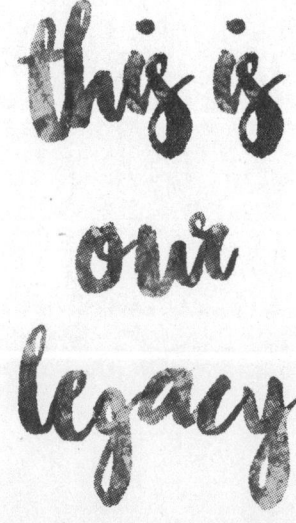

this is our legacy

What a wonderful time to be Catholic in the United States of America! Please join me once again praising the Lord by saying together a resounding amen:

Amen!

Thank you.

Questions for reflection and dialogue: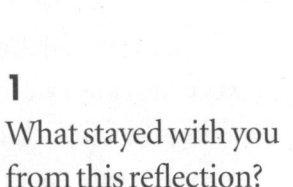

1
What stayed with you from this reflection?

2
What does it mean for you to be a missionary disciple of Jesus Christ?

3
In what ways does diversity (e.g., cultural, socio-economic, ideological) challenge how you live and practice your Christian faith with others?

4
If you were to reach out to one person or one group of people to tell them your story about the great things God has done in your life, who would this person or group be?

5
Is there anyone in your family or community who has stopped practicing his or her faith? What will you as a missionary disciple do to reach out to them?